THE STONE DOLL

OF

SISTER BRUTE

Story by Russell Hoban
Pictures by Lillian Hoban

A Snuggle & Read Story Book

AN AVON CAMELOT BOOK

AVON BOOKS
A division of
The Hearst Corporation
959 Eighth Avenue
New York, New York 10019

First Camelot Printing, October, 1980

For the whole original
Little Brute Family
from their loving
PAPA BRUTE

Once upon a time, before the Brute family
changed their name to Nice,
Sister Brute had nothing to love.

She had a mama and a papa.

She had a big brother and a baby brother.

"But I have nothing to love,"
said Sister Brute to her papa.
"May I have a doll?"

Papa growled and walked away.

"May I have a doll?"
Sister Brute asked her mama.

Mama gave her a stone.

Sister Brute drew a face on the stone.

Sister Brute made a dress for the stone.

She gave it tea parties in the woods.

She picked flowers for it, and
she named it Alice Brute Stone.

It was hard when she hugged it,
and it was heavy to carry, but
Sister Brute loved Alice Brute Stone.

One day Sister Brute took
Alice Brute Stone for a walk,
and met an ugly dog.

His hair was matted and dirty.
His hob-nailed boots were shabby and worn.
"Love me," said the dog to Sister Brute.

"No," said Sister Brute.

"I have my stone doll to love. Go away."

"Love me," said the dog,
"or I will kick you very hard."

"Then I will kick you back,"
said Sister Brute.

He kicked her
and she kicked him,
but the dog kicked harder
with his hob-nailed boots.

"Go away," said Sister Brute, and
she hurled her stone doll at the ugly dog.
"Nobody ever played dolls with me before,"
said the dog. "Now I know you love me."

So he followed her home with
Alice Brute Stone in his mouth,
and he kicked Sister Brute lovingly
all the way.

Now Sister Brute had Alice Brute Stone
to love, and she had the ugly dog with
the hob-nailed boots too.

But the doll was hard and heavy,
and the dog kept kicking.

One day Sister Brute
said to her mama,
"All I have is tiredness
and kicks and bruises."

"Maybe that is because you have
been loving only a hard stone
and a kicking dog," said Mama Brute.
"What else is there to love?"
said Sister Brute.
"I don't know," said Mama Brute.

Then she looked at Alice Brute Stone's face.
It was just like hers.
"You could love me," said Mama Brute,
"and I will give you soft hugs and
sing you lullabies."

"What will papa give me if I love him?"
said Sister Brute.
"Maybe kisses and knee rides," said Mama.

"What about Big Brother
and Baby Brother?" said Sister Brute.

"Smiles and string," said Mama.
"Rusty bolts and colored glass and turtles."

"Then I will try loving the whole family,"
said Sister Brute, "and I will keep on
loving Alice Brute Stone and
my ugly kicking dog too."

So she did.
Sister Brute loved them all,
and they loved her back, and she had
hugs and lullabies, kisses and knee rides,
smiles, string, colored glass and turtles and
kicks and bruises.
And she was happy.